Birthday Party

CELIA BERRIDGE

Kingfisher Books

Story by Angela Royston

Kingfisher Books, Grisewood & Dempsey Ltd,
Elsley House, 24–30 Great Titchfield Street,
London W1P 7AD

First published in 1988 by Kingfisher Books

Text copyright © Grisewood & Dempsey Ltd 1988
Illustrations copyright © Celia Berridge 1988

All rights reserved

BRITISH LIBRARY CATALOGUING IN PUBLICATION DATA
Berridge, Celia
   The birthday party.—(Stepping stones 1, 2, 3).
   1. Children's parties—Juvenile literature
   I. Title   II. Royston, Angela   III. Series
   793.2′1   GV1205
   ISBN: 0 86272 339 6

Edited by Vanessa Clarke
Editorial Assistant: Camilla Hallinan
Phototypeset by Southern Positives and
Negatives (SPAN), Lingfield, Surrey
Printed in Spain

It is my birthday party tomorrow and all my friends are coming. I am making hats for them to wear.

Mum and I are unpacking the shopping. Look at all the things we have bought for my party.

I can help Mum to make little cakes. Slip, slap! Slip, slap! It's hard work stirring everything together.

We are making biscuits too. I am using cutters to make different shapes. Look, this one is a gingerbread man.

We baked the little cakes in the oven. They smell good. Now they are cool and we can ice them. I like decorating the cakes too.

Hurrah! It's my birthday today. Mum has blown up all the balloons and we are hanging them up.

It is nearly time for the party and I am almost ready. Ouch! Don't pull my hair!.

My friends are arriving. Thank you for my present. I wonder what it is.

Mum has hidden packets of raisins for us to find. It's a treasure hunt. Let's look in the chair.

Now we are playing Pass the Parcel. When the music stops, you tear off a layer of paper. Right in the middle is a present.

Hurry up, and pass it on because the music is playing again.

Sam is pinning the tail on the donkey. He has a blindfold over his eyes so he can't see what he is doing. I wonder if he will pin the tail on the right place.

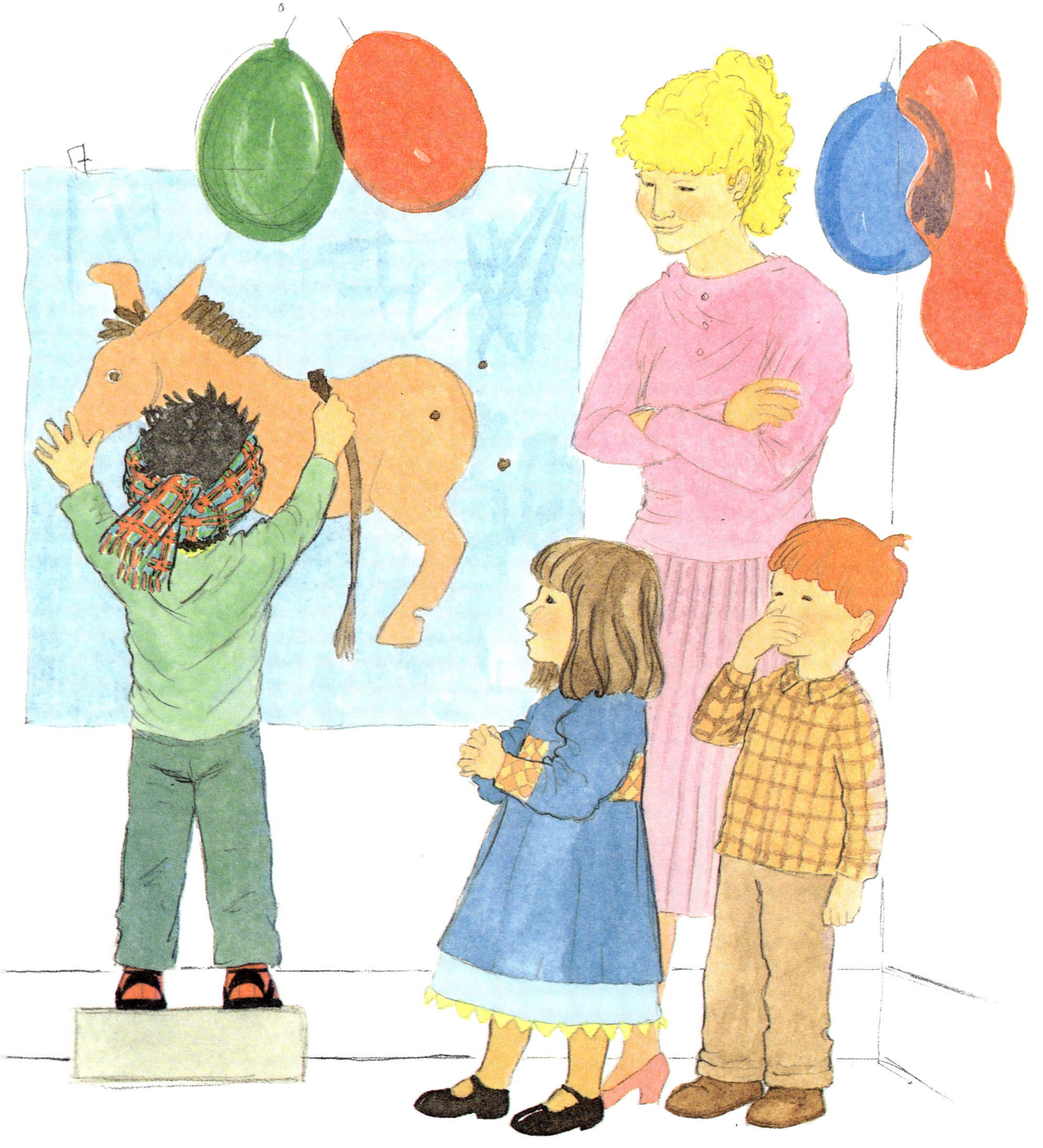

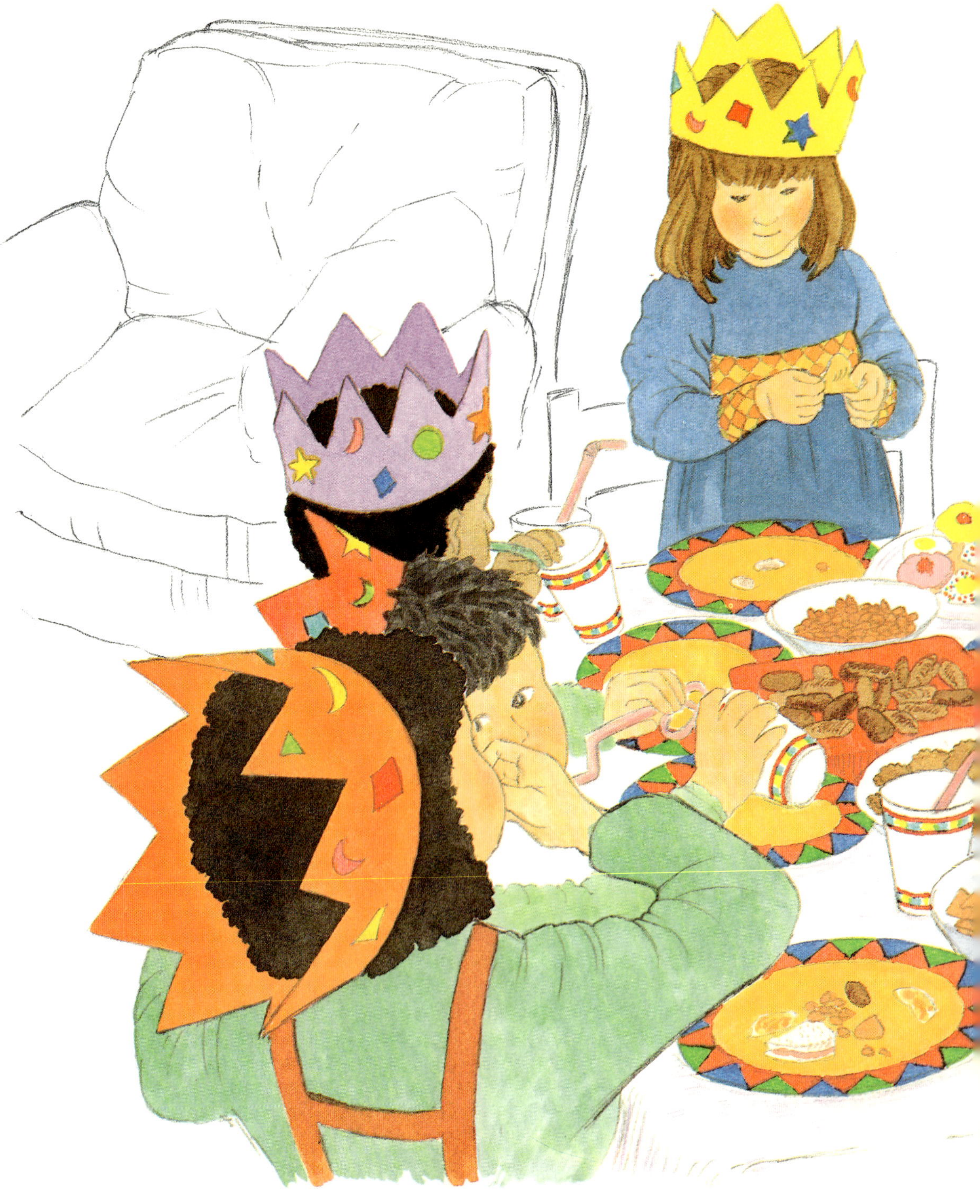

It is time for tea. I like the crisps and the little cakes. What shall I have next?

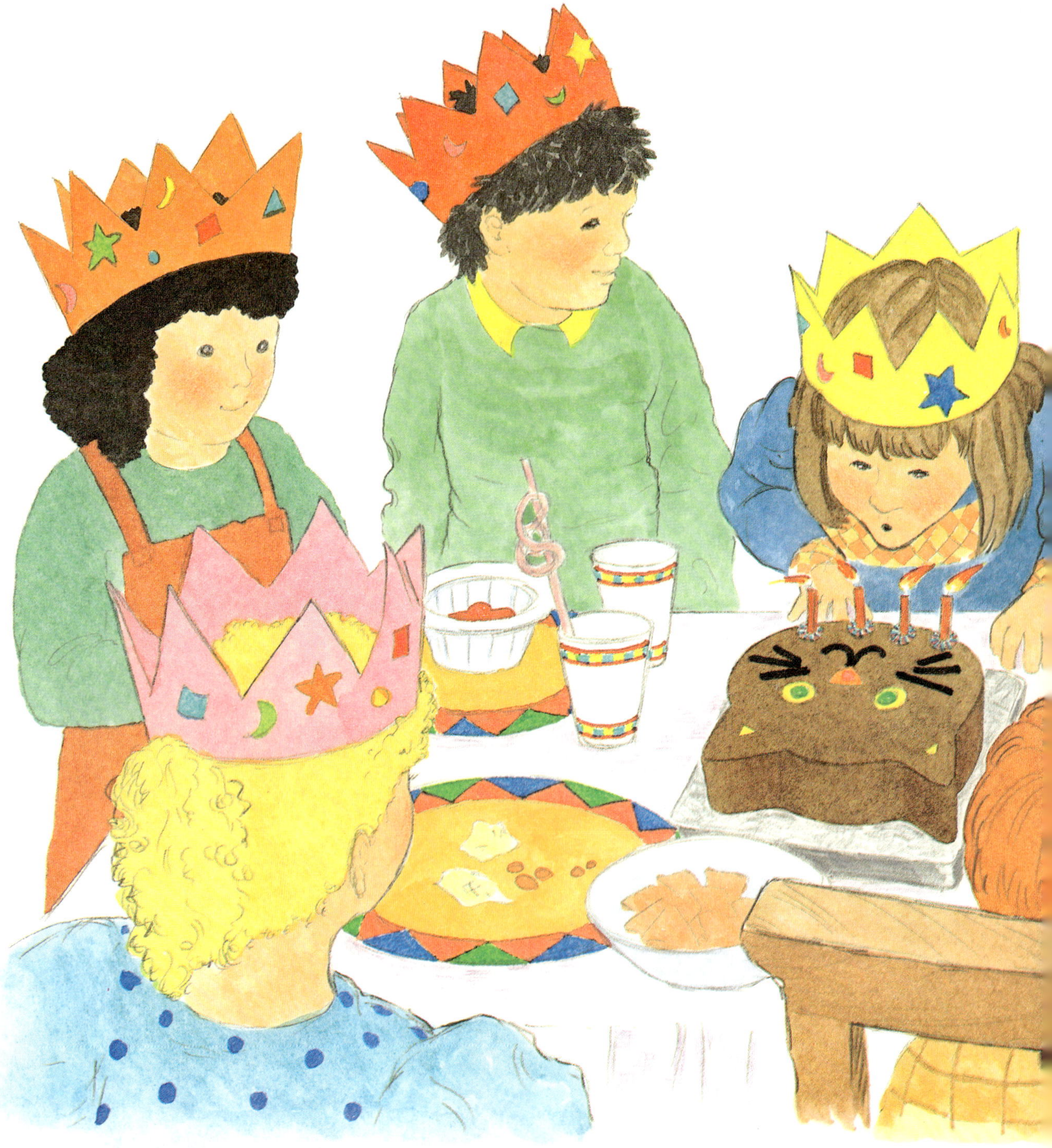

My birthday cake is a suprise. Look, it's a cat! Everyone sings Happy Birthday to me. I'm going to blow out the candles with one big puff.

Our fingers are sticky with icing so we are going to wash our hands.

Here is my cat on the bed. She doesn't like the noise of the party.

Let's play Musical Bumps. When Mum stops the music we all sit down. Bump! The last one down is out of the game. Then we all get up and dance, until the music stops again.

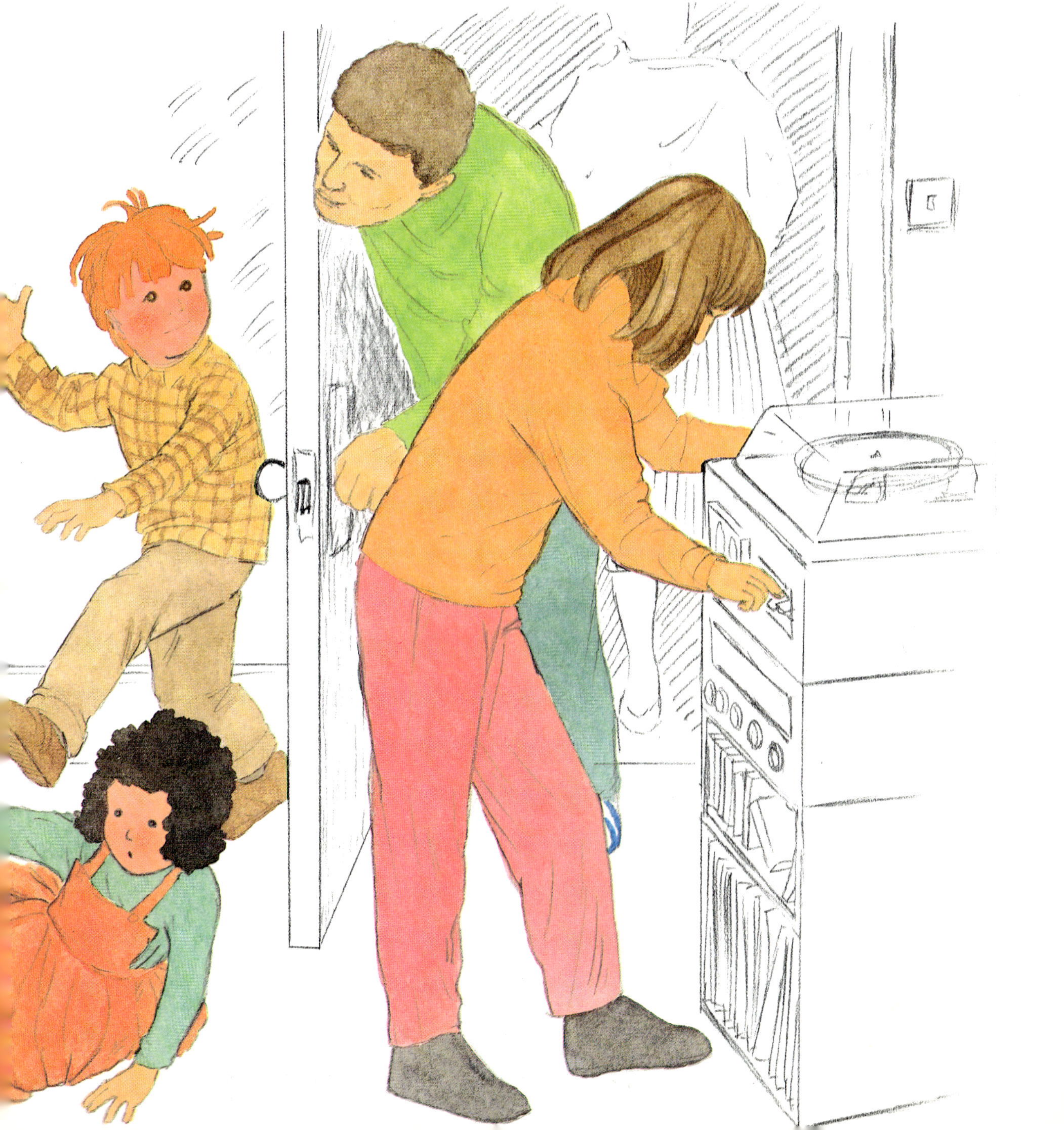

Oh dear, it is time for everyone to go home.
Thank you for coming to my party.
Goodbye.